Candle Wax

Shreya Panchmatia

BookLeaf Publishing

Presentation by *BookLeaf Publishing*

Web: www.bookleafpub.com

E-mail: info@bookleafpub.com

ISBN: 9789357211970

First edition 2023

ACKNOWLEDGEMENT

Ms M, Family & Friends

PREFACE

For me, I love to see how people read my own poetry; since only I know in that moment what I am writing about. The beautiful thing is that interpretations can vary wildly from person to person; but it can be something that they relate to in a different way than I may have intended. Hence, I usually write a bulk of my poetry from the eyes of others. Writing poetry from different perspectives is special. It allows you to walk inside someone else's skin; feel what they feel, think how they think. It allows you to explore emotions you yourself have never held. It allows you to blend both yours and their experiences into a beautifully crafted artistic piece.

The Garden

palettes and people
colours of pain
amber and april
evanesce in vain
crystal glass wine
dried tears and salty grains
picture the sunflower
old mustard and grey
dilemmas are real
black velvet and teal
dark icy red palms
trains surge to my arms
fingertips laced with blood
words that don't speak
thatched roof and a dove
a pit in my gut so bleak
those with no seeds
to water their growth
and me with no weeds
yet trudge and complain
the words wrap my ears
in vines and in tears
and staple my lips
with rope round my hips
could dare open a vein
to speak through the pain

but swallow the brave
{and i take it to my grave}

sometimes it's nice, tbh

{sometimes}
it's nice to cry
there's some comfort in tears
in the black of the night.
{sometimes}
it's nice to be vulnerable
shedding the layers
of the hard coated armour
i wear most days.
{sometimes}
it's nice to lie down
and just look at the empty light
contemplating life
until your eyes go dry
and then you wet them with your tears
just so you can keep them alive
and find comfort within the blankets
and feel special when you hide.

Oh April Wind

for a heart so fragile
wintery warmth healed the wounds
with scars of motherly desire
and shower holds winter blues
as tears like rain water fall
and sweat like water fountains spray
where young hearts with love smile
and winter cold ever so chill
with shiver comes the light
and furry coats with feather duster wool
a sneeze a call towards the mist
upon the grey roads of tarmac grey ice
the yellow umbrella like icicles hang
metallic chugs of tractor black coals
sink inside my lungs the fumes of hope
and hiss and hum and bring me to a wheeze
so i say goodbye to the winter holding breeze
where snow in April and hot Christmas days
non plastic bottles and wrappes just another
craze
from garbage dump to feather duster canes
forever shall the fortitude of our past reign
and hang like trees like paper banners of our
voice
fade from my fingers until i have no choice

i stand above your grave, oh April wind
hold me close
{i knew that they would win}

Cerberus

find my calling
the shriek of an angel cry
waving through the wind
and desert water dry
crusty fingertips meet light
with shining flicker of hope
fear of the shadow behind
forging blood to cope
cannot stop with the thoughts
seconds wasted with their pain
imprint my signature on my palm
and let the hungry ghosts reign
where past meets present
a simple shake of a hand
and whistling with the rain
to before the wind understand
why my tears are lost and frozen
my heart black and broken
my callings so loud they are silent
my hands are none but violent
still could shake unto the floor
until the blue lights wake me no more
the sorrow that usually wanes
could it be worse than physical pain?
or could i clutch the ends and tails

of painless peace?
{will this feeling prevail?}

Ode to Shame

let me love the part that hates me
that makes it thunder on rainy days
that makes the sun set when it should be rising
that makes the days shrink like a wintery haze.
let me hold the part that hates me
in a basket with a blanket inside
i will protect it with some covers
and stroke its hair goodnight.
let me let the part that hates me
hate me with free will;
for if i hate the part that hates me
then hate will freeze me still.
like wintery ice on heavy days,
the sky falls when it should still be light;
i miss the rich smelling grass and flower blooms,
so i hide inside a corner that doesn't exist.
i shame every inch of my soul when i'm alone,
then i hate the part of me that shames myself.
i wither away because everything seems "so
bad"
whereas if i held shame by their hand
i could make them hold mine back
i could help them find their own self love
so that it helps me live inside mine.
for shame, i owe it to you

for being with me since day one
you truly are a loyal friend,
there beside me during my toughest moments.
to shame,
i don't hate you anymore;
i promise i will cherish your touch.
i will let you be exactly who you are,
and i'll help you find some love.

Breakfast

empty days
wane away
as time fades from the grip of my palm
trudge through the layers of smoke
wishful words as they spoke
a foggy path appears
broken stones
sandy dunes of muddy cones
wasting all my tears
watering the flowers which do not exist
trace the veins of watery rivers
proceed as they become shackles on my wrists
sunset rivers and bacon dinners
where cowbell gibberish are the winners.

Toast.

Informal Folk

a touch on mythical grass
to split the Earth and swallow glass
i held their hands so tightly
to hold them back from their fantasy
Cut from the inside,
swallowed whole from the out,
supernatural waters holding the ground solid
piecing cracks puzzled together
take me by the hand
we will walk to the light together
it's seeping through the branches now
it's rustling through the trees
take my by the hand, i tell you
simply kiss away the world
Cupid will love you forever
from cracks to whiskey lawns.

Kingdom of Swift Abuse

I have bowed down
to the demon
which exists
as a shadow of my soul.
Snatched behind
the shadowed debut
of crystal covers blow.
the leaves distorted
as the river ebbs and flows.
malice and treachery
strangling the communion
of twenty sisters there.
they stand hand in hand
bullets to their heads
wishing they were dead.
could this be the day
where breath no longer coils?

in my mind a storm,
a whistle in the air.
churning fear;
it strokes my face
and it pacifies the demon.
we are now face to face.
This is my place.

Hand held on handle,
and trust on the trigger.
Index curled inside,
wishing i were thinner.
A slow motion murder
shown to me in the mirror.

Blood on my hands.

squint no more.
I must see the damage I have caused.
Wide open are my eyes,
yet they pay no remorse.

Cowardly love
for complex evil deeds.
One after the other -
I am on a spree.

dear younger me

heavy heads and heavy minds
there was so much to think about
all the time
the person in the mirror
she cried all the time
but hid from the light
and closed all the blinds
she'd curl in a ball
behind her bed
staring at her phone
contemplating what had been said
rocking back and forth
fingers in her mouth
swaying side to side
trying to comprehend life.
the books she would read
about demons and fairies
provided comfort in tough times
even though they were lies.
they were a more special world
better than the one she endured
and so she'd smile as the
crisp pages folded.
the stories she told in her head
was better than anything undead.

she was too busy all focussed on the smoke
that she couldn't see the colourful sparks.
she'd blow out the candle
and we wouldn't see
the young woman
she would soon grow up to be.

Memory

I remember her tiny little flat,
and the sofa in which we all sat.
The bathroom behind the sliding door;
the fluffy carpet laid on the floor.
Behind the sofa lay her bed,
As a child - "I want to live here!" is what I said.

She always greeted us with a smile,
So happy we were there - even for a little while.
Maybe I didn't always understand what she
would say,
But I would still enjoy the company, I would
still enjoy the stay.

She would hug me, smother me with love,
as I'm sure she still does now, just from above.
I never really understood the joy she would feel,
from a simple hour of our presence - her joy was
so real.
She would talk, she would laugh and even play
with us all,
I remember all of the games from when I was so
small.

Did I think she was mortal? Did I realise her worth?
Did I notice the fact she loved me right from my birth?
Did I know that I'd miss her only once she was gone?
Did I know of her past and how she always marched on?

I am lucky enough to be showered with these memories, these thoughts.
Including the chocolate we would get as we left - the ones that she bought.
Those chocolates were the highlight of my visist as a child,
And to just see her once more I wish for - just for a while.

And it hurts that she's gone
We all loved her so dearly
But we know that she's strong
And in the sky, as a star
We'll see her so clearly.

In loving memory of S.

dear paranoia

your eyes are implanted on me
i can feel your stares
everywhere i walk
flooding through the air.
i cannot escape your glance
as you judge my every move
your silent whispers
crawling through my ears
i wince in pain
as they sprawl and crawl
through my veins.
feeling alone
walking across the grassy hills
and snakey paths
leading me to nowhere.
you'll pierce me again
with your dagger driven eyes
until the tears run dry
{weightless in a river}

Judy's string

my heart falling through my fingers
the blood soaking my palms
watching myself melt all over the tarmac
drip dripping with the seconds turn turning
the heavy scent of rusty blades
and bitter tasting velvet spades
dig digging beneath my feet
sink sinking into the ground
like quick sand, i am swallowed
numb minded and quiet faced
the grey soil called concrete
like bendy roads under my skin
the silence pierces me from within
barefoot on a soaked gravel ridden floor
walking like slack string being pulled towards a
light
crystal balls and rainwater save me no more
for i walk into the sand, grains between my toes
where the salty waves tease my feet
bit by bit, crawling around my skin, tenacious
water reaching my chin, breathless out and in
{panic no more} a hostile voice speaks
{for i will take you by the hand
promise you the world
whisper in your ear

and like puppet
~ you'll be mine}

compass

i'm indulging in a fantasy
lying awake with you on my mind
holding onto corners of a circle
going round and round
in an endless cycle of addiction
nanoparticles of your hopeless love
smother me relentless.

losing a friend

swallowed into the pretence
remember what we were then
i type the questions but never press send
through my fingertips falls a friend

overthinking takes your place
from shaking my hand
to suffocating my face
endless thoughts and endless cycles
sinking back into the past for a while

the words and letters all float in my head
i type the questions but never press send
so they linger;
bitterly dormant at my tongue
the past, it soaks me;
i'm analysing what went wrong

swallowed into the past now
fighting for every last breath i can forge
the questions;
they crawl their way into my lungs
they write their own answers then leave;
i'm left numb

floating in the past like a corpse in the ocean
alone in the dark blue, poisoned with solitude
when the buoyancy wanes, finally the flame will
flicker out
no longer do the questions fester;
the self-written answers have taken their place
and they sink me much faster

yet i fade at a much slower pace.

after it all ends

are you smiling?
or spending days crying?
exhausted baffled and upset
uneasy unsure and hopeful
grappling hold of slack ropes
hanging down from the moon
crumbling in the stress you built up
but forgot to break down
forgot that there's an end
to be honest i didn't realise
how long the walk would be
from the edge of a balcony
to home.

supposed to be a weight lifted
so that i can carry myself.
supposed to be smiling
after the stress.
did i panic enough?
was i too relaxed?

thought provoking
candle choking
i can't breathe
my heart is broken

with piece of my wimpy eyed
mona lisa drawings
stuck losely on a grey painted wall.

listening to my hollow music songs.

glue

i never really understood anyway
days would wane
without the pain.
instead, it was left there;
in the scorching sun
so it can melt itself inside me
solder it to my heart
hold me captive
{like an art}

Home

Home.
Where the motherly love lingers,
softly bespoken into the moonlit sky.
As the darkness befalls upon me,
I smile at the days gone by.
I have spent time here,
singing softly with the breeze and
here at home is where I am protected;
from the forests and the trees.

climate

metallic whining
burning air
abusing love
corrupting life
but we have the power
to rid of the whining
but we sit idle
passively destroying.

Tears in My Mask

there was terror in my eyes
and in my wavering lips
i wanted to run and hide
{disappear into the mist}
tears folded over my pupils
fear cradled me in its arms
my emotions weighted against my chest
{this is all a dream}
i told myself
{this is a test}

a test to see if my strength will carry me through
but yet weeks on
i find myself holding onto the corners
folding the covers
turning away from the universe
{and saying goodbye to the others}

moon

she said
fire was her language
and the moon;
her companion.

Gone

hold me like the wind cries in its sleep
cold in the river running away from me
hiding beneath the surface
to erupt behind the trees
growing behind our thoughts
overshadowing our minds
crying forever
tears that trace
my cheeks
they embed
themselves
within
my skin
so i peel
away
until
i am
gone.

www.ingramcontent.com/pod-product-compliance
Lightning Source LLC
Chambersburg PA
CBHW051750130826
49812CB00033B/1079
9789357211970